WOULD YOU RATHER

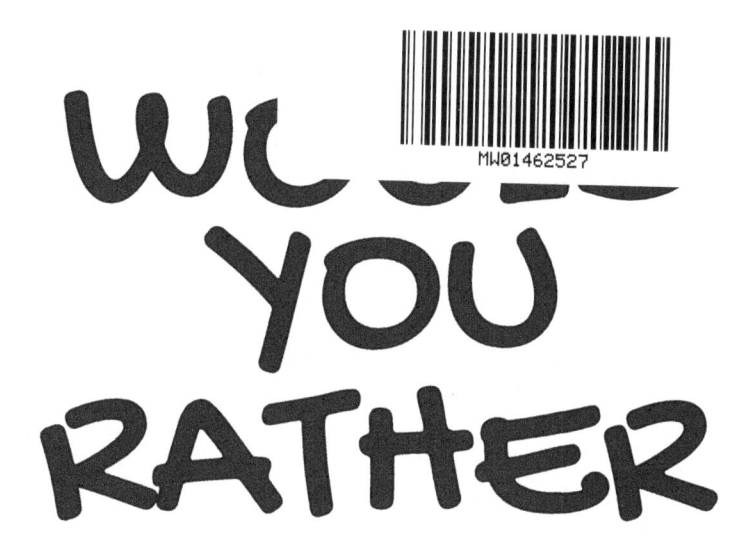

GAME BOOK

For Kids 6-12 Years Old

CRAZY JOKES
AND CREATIVE SCENARIOS
FOR SPACE FANS

Lucky Sammy

Copyright © 2020 by Lucky Sammy

All rights reserved

ISBN: 9798684209116

No part of this publication may be reproduced, distributed, or transmitted
in any form or by any means without the prior written permission of the publisher.

The cover image is designed by Freepik
www.freepik.com

CONTENTS

HOW TO PLAY?..4

1. SOLAR SYSTEM...5

2. SPACE TRAVEL..21

3. ASTRONAUTICS..37

4. PLANET EARTH..53

5. ALIENS..69

6. UNIVERSE..85

7. NIGHT SKY...101

HOW TO PLAY?

YOU WILL NEED TWO TO THREE PLAYERS, SO CHOOSE YOUR FRIENDS, PEERS, SIBLINGS, COUSINS OR PARENTS AND GUARDIANS WISELY!

THE QUESTIONS SHOULD BE ASKED TO THE WHOLE GROUP AND NOT TO EACH PLAYER. IT IS A FUN, INTRIGUING, STIMULATING, AND EXCITING GAME WHERE YOU CAN FIND OUT SECRETS ABOUT YOUR FRIENDS & FAMILY.

INSTINCTS VS THOUGHTS, THINKING VS FEELING, EMOTIONS VS INTELLECT, BELIEFS AND PHILOSOPHY VS LOGIC AND REASON, DISCOVERING KNOWLEDGE VS SIMPLE FUN; THIS GAME HAS A RANGE OF EFFECTS!

TRY AND RELY ON YOUR INSTINCTUAL FEELINGS AND "GUT" RESPONSES. WHAT INSTANTLY COMES TO MIND? THIS IS THE WAY YOU SHOULD ANSWER. YOU CAN USE A TIMER OR HOURGLASS, IF YOU AND YOUR FELLOW PLAYERS NEED SOME STRUCTURE.

ENJOY!

SOLAR SYSTEM

WOULD YOU RATHER

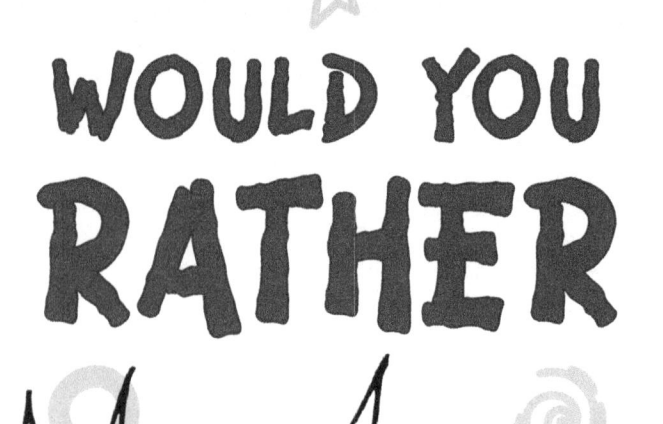

FLY THROUGH THE RINGS OF SATURN
OR
VISIT THE ASTEROID BELT?

WALK ON THE BOILING SURFACE OF VENUS
OR
SINK THROUGH THE GAS OF SATURN?

WOULD YOU RATHER

DISCOVER A NEW PLANET
OR
LIVE ON THE MOON?

VISIT THE GREAT RED SPOT ON JUPITER
OR
OLYMPUS MONS ON MARS?

WOULD YOU RATHER

MAKE A TRIP TO THE SUN
OR
VISIT THE ICY SURFACE OF PLUTO?

SEE THE SUN AS IT FORMED
OR
WATCH THE MOON BE CREATED?

WOULD YOU RATHER

WATCH THE EARTH ORBIT AROUND THE SUN
OR
THE SUN ORBIT AROUND EARTH?

HAVE A PLANET NAMED AFTER YOU
OR
RENAME MERCURY AFTER YOUR PET?

WOULD YOU RATHER

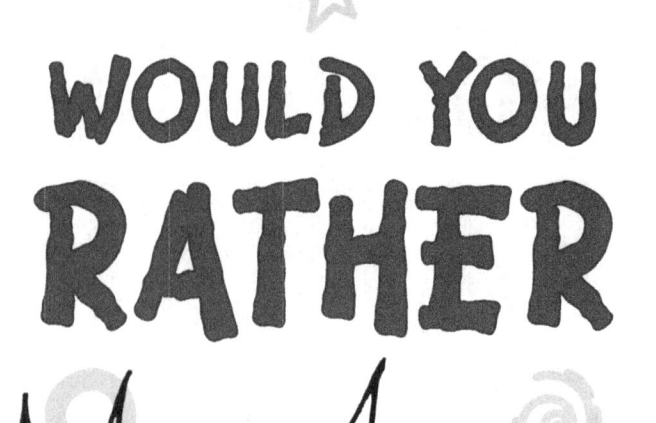

VISIT THE SITE OF A SOLAR ECLIPSE
OR
A LUNAR ECLIPSE?

GET A TAN ON MERCURY
OR
BUILD A SNOWMAN ON NEPTUNE?

WOULD YOU RATHER

LIVE ON A MOON OF SATURN
OR
ON A COLONY ON THE MOON?

TURN JUPITER BRIGHT PINK
OR
MAKE THE CRATERS ON
THE MOON PURPLE?

WOULD YOU RATHER

LIVE ON A SUPER COLD PLANET LIKE URANUS,
OR
A SUPER HOT PLANET LIKE VENUS?

LIVE IN THE DEEPEST CRATER IN THE SOLAR SYSTEM
OR
THE TALLEST MOUNTAIN IN THE SOLAR SYSTEM?

WOULD YOU RATHER

GATHER SPACE ROCKS FROM
THE ASTEROID BELT
OR
THE KUIPER BELT?

VISIT A VOLCANO ON VENUS
OR
ON THE MOONS OF JUPITER?

WOULD YOU RATHER

DRINK ICE WATER FROM MARS
OR
THE MOON?

BE IN A HURRICANE ON EARTH
OR
ON JUPITER?

WOULD YOU RATHER

LIVE ON A DESERTED ISLAND ON EARTH
OR
BE STRANDED ON AN ASTEROID?

LIVE ON A PLANET WITH NO ATMOSPHERE,
LIKE MERCURY,
OR
ONE WITH TOO MUCH ATMOSPHERE,
LIKE VENUS?

WOULD YOU RATHER

NAME ASTEROIDS AFTER ALL OF YOUR FRIENDS
OR
GIVE ALL OF YOUR FRIENDS A PIECE OF A METEOR?

MAKE FRIENDS WITH THE MARS CURIOSITY ROVER
OR
THE VOYAGER PROBE?

WOULD YOU RATHER

VISIT THE MOON ON VACATION
OR
GO LIVE ON MERCURY?

SEE A VOLCANO ON MARS
OR
AN ICE STORM ON SATURN?

WOULD YOU RATHER

EAT A PIECE OF MOON ROCK
OR
A PIECE OF PLUTO?

BE ABLE TO SEE THE SOLAR SYSTEM
WITHOUT A TELESCOPE BUT NOT THE EARTH
OR
BE ABLE TO SEE THE WHOLE EARTH
BUT NOT THE SOLAR SYSTEM?

WOULD YOU RATHER

BE A SATELLITE ORBITING THE EARTH
OR
A PROBE SEARCHING THE WHOLE GALAXY?

HAVE DOZENS OF MOONS ORBITING AROUND YOU THAT ARE SMALL
OR
ONE MOON THE SAME SIZE AS YOU?

WOULD YOU RATHER

MEMORIZE A MAP OF THE MOON
OR
A MAP OF MERCURY?

TRAVEL NORTH TO SEE THE AURORA BOREALIS
OR
STARGAZE FOR AN HOUR TO SEE A SHOOTING STAR?

SPACE TRAVEL

WOULD YOU RATHER

TRAVEL TO A GALAXY FAR AWAY
OR
EXPLORE THE MILKY WAY?

VISIT THE SUN
OR
A STAR FAR AWAY?

WOULD YOU RATHER

VISIT A PLANET THAT IS JUST LIKE EARTH
OR
ONE THAT BREAKS THE LAWS OF PHYSICS?

TRAVEL FASTER THAN THE SPEED OF LIGHT
OR
TIMETRAVEL TO THE PAST?

WOULD YOU RATHER

DISCOVER WATER ON A PLANET IN THE SOLAR SYSTEM
OR
LIFE ON A PLANET VERY FAR AWAY?

LIVE ON A PLANET THAT'S ALL WATER
OR
A PLANET THAT'S ALL ROCKS?

WOULD YOU RATHER

GET SUCKED INTO A BLACK HOLE
OR
CRASH INTO A STAR?

BE ABLE TO BREATHE WITHOUT A SPACESUIT
OR
FLY WITHOUT A ROCKET SHIP?

WOULD YOU RATHER

WATCH THE SUN EXPLODING
OR
WATCH IT FORMING?

LIVE ON A PLANET WITH SO MUCH GRAVITY YOU CAN'T STAND UP
OR
ONE WITH SO LITTLE GRAVITY THAT YOU FLOAT?

WOULD YOU RATHER

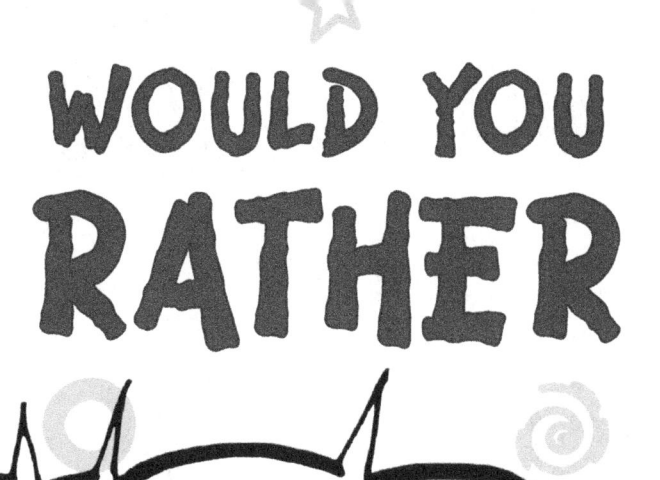

VISIT THE BIGGEST STAR IN THE GALAXY
OR
THE SMALLEST ONE?

WATCH THE SOLAR SYSTEM FORM
OR
THE SUN EXPLODE?

WOULD YOU RATHER

MAKE THE SUN CHANGE COLOR
TO BRIGHT PINK
OR
TO BLACK?

FIND A PLANET WITH ONLY ANIMALS
OR
A PLANET WITH ONLY PLANTS?

WOULD YOU RATHER

BE ABLE TO TELEPORT FROM PLANET TO PLANET
OR
BE ABLE TO BREATHE IN ANY ATMOSPHERE?

USE A SPACESHIP WITH ARTIFICIAL GRAVITY
OR
A SHIP WITH NO GRAVITY?

WOULD YOU RATHER

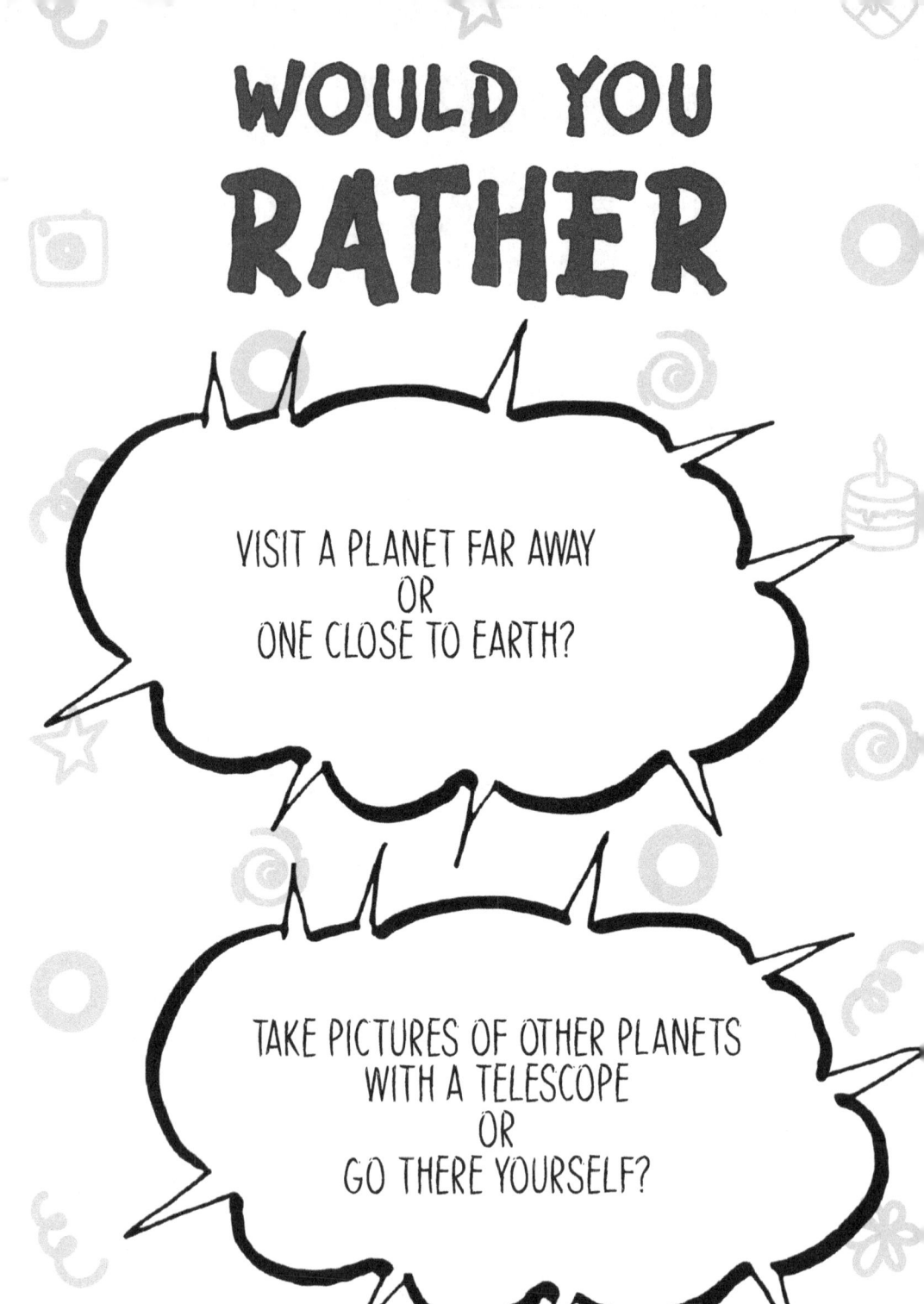

VISIT A PLANET FAR AWAY
OR
ONE CLOSE TO EARTH?

TAKE PICTURES OF OTHER PLANETS
WITH A TELESCOPE
OR
GO THERE YOURSELF?

WOULD YOU RATHER

TRAVEL THROUGH SPACE WITH YOUR PET
OR
YOUR SIBLINGS?

DRINK WATER FROM A FARAWAY PLANET
OR
EAT THE VEGETABLES THAT GROW ON IT?

WOULD YOU RATHER

LIVE ON A SPACESHIP
OR
LIVE ON ANOTHER PLANET?

LIVE IN A SOLAR SYSTEM WITH
THREE STARS
OR
A PLANET WITH THREE MOONS?

WOULD YOU RATHER

DISCOVER A NEW PLANET
OR
A NEW STAR?

FIND A PLANET THAT'S FLAT AS PAPER
OR
ONE THAT'S SHAPED LIKE A DONUT?

WOULD YOU RATHER

LIVE ON THE FIRST PLANET YOU LAND ON
OR
MOVE FROM PLANET TO PLANET EVERY DAY?

VISIT A SOLAR SYSTEM WITH ONLY GAS GIANT PLANETS
OR
A SYSTEM WITH ONLY ROCKY PLANETS?

WOULD YOU RATHER

FIND A NEW ELEMENT ON ANOTHER PLANET
OR
DISCOVER LIFE ON ONE?

LIVE IN A SPACE STATION AND GO TO WORK ON THE SURFACE
OR
WORK AT A SPACE STATION AND LIVE ON THE SURFACE?

WOULD YOU RATHER

VISIT NEW GALAXIES IN THE PAST
OR
IN THE FUTURE?

DISCOVER A PLANET RULED BY CATS
OR
ONE RULED BY DOGS?

ASTRONAUTICS

WOULD YOU RATHER

BE THE FIRST PERSON ON THE MOON
OR
THE FIRST PERSON ON MARS?

BE THE CAPTAIN OF A SPACESHIP
OR
THE PILOT?

WOULD YOU RATHER

USE A SHIP WITH FASTER THAN LIGHT TRAVEL AND TRAVEL FOR A FEW YEARS
OR
BE ON A SLOWER SHIP AND SLEEP FOR THE WHOLE JOURNEY?

COMMAND A BATTLESHIP ARMED WITH MISSILES
OR
A SCIENCE SHIP WITH ALL OF THE LATEST EXPERIMENTS?

WOULD YOU RATHER

FLOAT THROUGH SPACE IN A SPACESUIT
OR
IN A ONE-PERSON SPACESHIP?

BE IN A SPACESHIP WITH NO WINDOWS
OR
ONE WITH CONSTANT TURBULENCE?

WOULD YOU RATHER

LIVE IN A SPACE STATION THAT ONLY ORBITS ONE PLANET
OR
ON A SHIP THAT TRAVELS ALL THE TIME?

TAKE A SHIP TO THE SUN
OR
TO PLUTO?

WOULD YOU RATHER

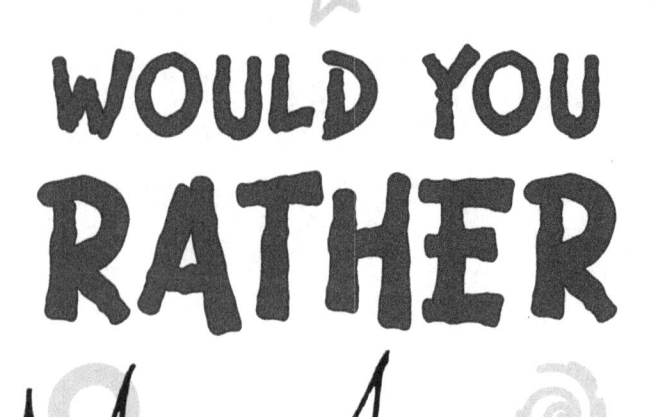

WEAR A SPACESUIT THAT IS
BRIGHT ORANGE
OR
LIME GREEN?

DO A SPACEWALK ON THE INTERNATIONAL
SPACE STATION
OR
WALK ON THE MOON?

WOULD YOU RATHER

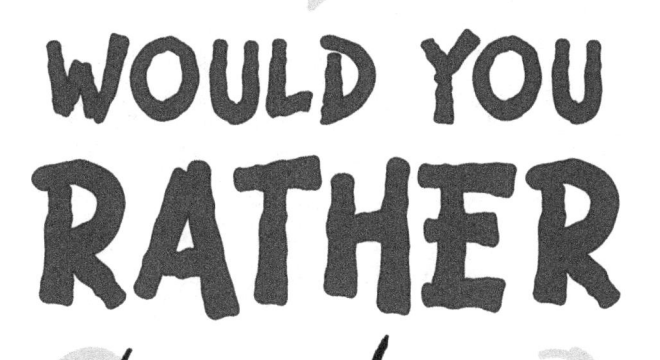

PILOT A SPACESHIP THAT LOOKS LIKE A MINIVAN
OR
ONE THAT LOOKS LIKE A GOLF CART?

BE A MEMBER OF THE CREW OF THE ISS
OR
THE FIRST MISSION TO MARS?

WOULD YOU RATHER

LIVE ON A COLONY ON THE MOON
OR
ON MARS?

VISIT A PLANET IN PERSON
OR
COMMAND A ROVER FROM EARTH?

WOULD YOU RATHER

GROW UP IN SPACE
OR
RAISE YOUR FUTURE KIDS IN SPACE?

HAVE YOUR PARENTS BECOME ASTRONAUTS
OR
SEND YOUR PET TO THE SPACE STATION?

WOULD YOU RATHER

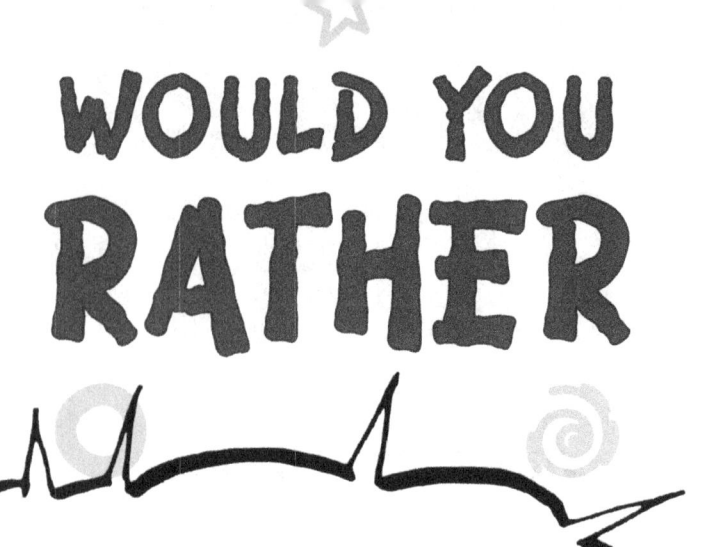

GO TO SCHOOL ON A MOON COLONY
OR
ON A FARAWAY PLANET?

EAT FREEZEDRIED ASTRONAUT FOOD
OR
JELLO FOR EVERY MEAL?

WOULD YOU RATHER

BE IN THE CONTROL CENTER IN HOUSTON
OR
AT THE ROCKET LAUNCH IN FLORIDA?

BE THE PHYSICIST MAKING ALL OF THE CALCULATIONS FOR THE SPACESHIP
OR
THE ENGINEER PUTTING EVERYTHING TOGETHER?

WOULD YOU RATHER

FLY THROUGH A FIELD OF ASTEROIDS
OR
THE CLOUD OF A NEBULA?

BE AN ASTRONAUT YOURSELF
OR
WATCH OTHERS AS ASTRONAUTS WHILE YOU HAVE ANOTHER JOB?

WOULD YOU RATHER

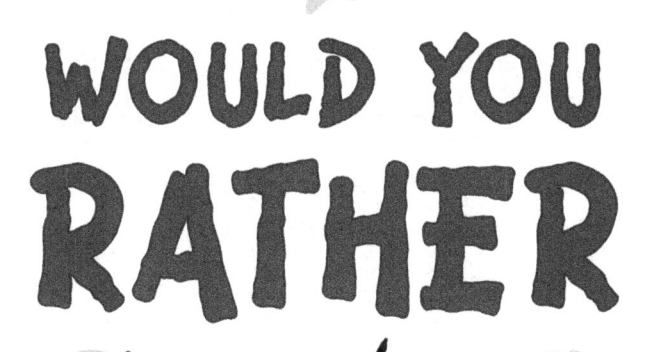

PILOT A ROCKETSHIP THAT CAN ONLY FLY LEFT AND RIGHT
OR
ONE THAT CAN ONLY FLY UP AND DOWN?

COMMAND A SHIP WHERE THE ONLY CREW IS OTHER KIDS
OR
WHERE YOU'RE THE ONLY KID?

WOULD YOU RATHER

FLY A SPACESHIP WITH NO BRAKES
OR
A SPACESHIP WITH NO ENGINE?

HAVE YOUR CAPTAIN BE A ROBOT
OR
AN ALIEN?

WOULD YOU RATHER

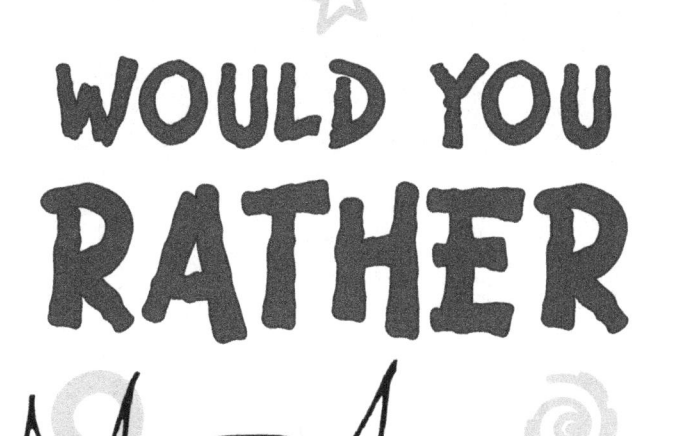

DO ALL OF YOUR SPACE TRAVEL IN OUR SOLAR SYSTEM
OR
IN ANOTHER GALAXY?

DISCOVER A PLANET WITH NO LIFE AT ALL
OR
A PLANET RUN BY SPIDERS?

WOULD YOU RATHER

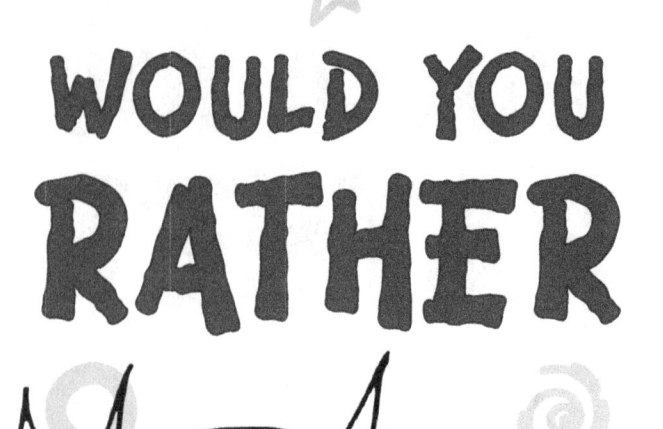

HAVE YOUR SPACESHIP TRAVEL SLOWLY BUT YOU ALWAYS KNOW WHERE YOU'RE GOING
OR
TRAVEL THROUGH A WORMHOLE WITH NO IDEA WHAT YOUR DESTINATION IS?

COMMAND A SPACESHIP
OR
A COLONY ON ANOTHER PLANET?

PLANET EARTH

WOULD YOU RATHER

VISIT THE TOP OF MOUNT EVEREST
OR
THE BOTTOM OF THE MARIANAS TRENCH?

LIVE IN THE AMAZON RAINFOREST
OR
THE SAHARA DESERT?

WOULD YOU RATHER

LIVE IN THE NORTH POLE WITH POLAR BEARS
OR
IN THE SOUTH POLE WITH PENGUINS?

DISCOVER A NEW SPECIES OF PLANT
OR
A NEW SPECIES OF ANIMAL?

WOULD YOU RATHER

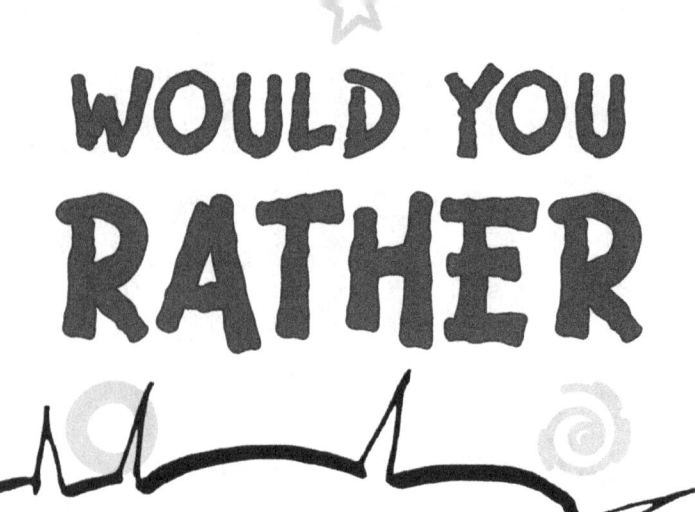

BE A BUG FOR A DAY
OR
A RODENT FOR A DAY?

LEARN TO CLIMB TREES
OR
LEARN TO SCUBA DIVE?

WOULD YOU RATHER

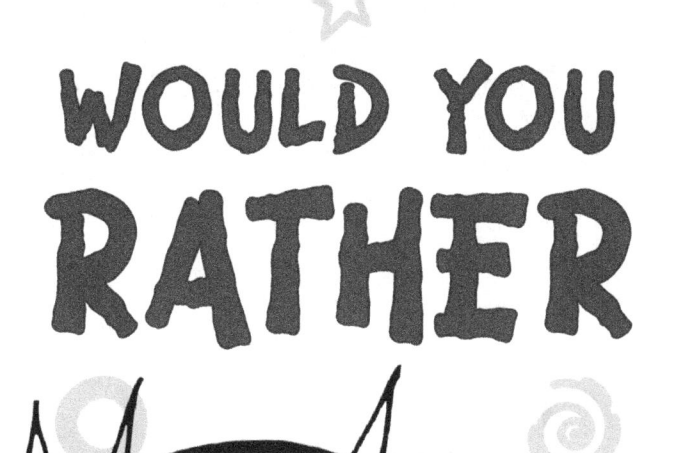

EAT AN EDIBLE FLOWER THAT TASTES LIKE CANDY
OR
AN EDIBLE BUG THAT TASTES LIKE CHIPS?

BE ABLE TO BREATHE UNDERWATER
OR
FLOAT IN THE AIR?

WOULD YOU RATHER

BE ABLE TO DRINK SEAWATER FROM ANY OCEAN
OR
EAT ROCKS FROM ANY CONTINENT?

LIVE ON A FARM WITH NO ONE AROUND
OR
IN A BIG CITY WITH NO NATURE CLOSE BY?

WOULD YOU RATHER

TIME TRAVEL 100 YEARS TO THE FUTURE
OR
100 YEARS TO THE PAST?

TIME TRAVEL TO MEET THE DINOSAURS
OR
MEET CAVEMEN?

WOULD YOU RATHER

LEARN TO RIDE AN ELEPHANT
OR
LEARN HOW TO SURF WAVES ON THE OCEAN?

SCUBA DIVE IN THE GREAT BARRIER REEF
OR
SKI IN THE MOUNTAINS OF COLORADO?

WOULD YOU RATHER

HIKE UP A STEEP MOUNTAIN TRAIL
OR
USE A MOUNTAIN BIKE TO GO UP THAT TRAIL?

WALK A MILE IN NATURE EVERY DAY
OR
DRIVE 10 MILES IN OPEN FIELDS EVERY DAY?

WOULD YOU RATHER

HAVE A NATIONAL PARK NAMED AFTER YOU
OR
HAVE A MOUNTAIN NAMED AFTER YOU?

DRINK THE WATER FROM A GLACIER
OR
EAT A PLANT FROM A RAINFOREST?

WOULD YOU RATHER

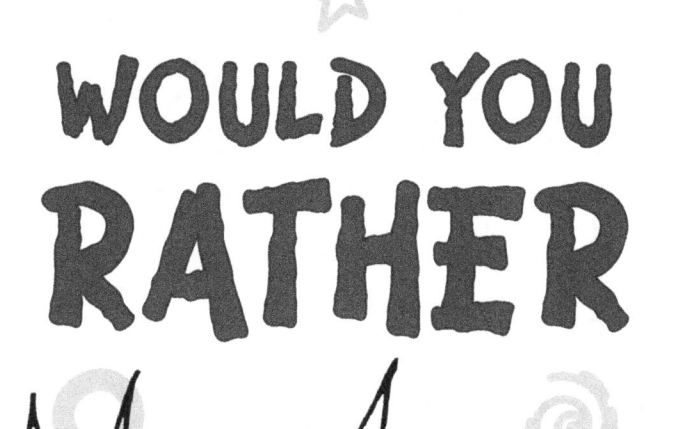

TRAVEL TO THE ANCIENT RUINS OF CIVILIZATIONS IN EGYPT
OR
IN MEXICO?

GET TURNED INTO A FLOWER IN A BOTANICAL GARDEN
OR
GET TURNED INTO A FISH IN AN AQUARIUM?

WOULD YOU RATHER

LIVE IN A HOUSE ON YOUR OWN PRIVATE ISLAND
OR
LIVE ON THE BEACH IN A POPULAR CITY?

ONLY BE ABLE TO DRINK WATER FROM SPRINGS
OR
ONLY BE ABLE TO EAT FOOD GROWN IN YOUR BACKYARD?

WOULD YOU RATHER

TRAVEL ACROSS THE WORLD BY FLYING
OR
BY DIGGING A TUNNEL UNDERGROUND?

DISCOVER THE REMAINS OF A DINOSAUR
OR
THE RUINS OF AN ANCIENT CIVILIZATION?

WOULD YOU RATHER

MAKE FRIENDS WITH A DOLPHIN
OR
A BUFFALO?

LIVE ON A FARM WITH COWS
OR
IN AN ORCHARD WITH APPLE TREES?

WOULD YOU RATHER

GO TO THE BOTTOM OF THE OCEAN
OR
TO THE BOTTOM OF THE DEEPEST VALLEY ON LAND?

DIG A HOLE TO THE CENTER OF THE EARTH
OR
TAKE A SHIP TO THE TOP OF THE ATMOSPHERE?

WOULD YOU RATHER

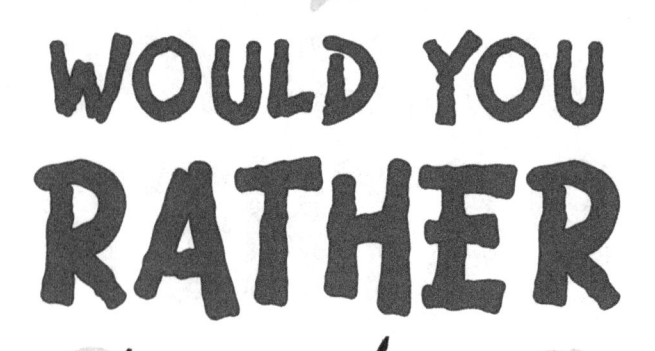

TURN EVERY PIGEON IN THE WORLD BRIGHT RED
OR
MAKE ALL BUTTERFLIES FIVE FEET TALL?

INVENT FLYING CARS
OR
INVENT A WAY TO TELEPORT?

ALIENS

WOULD YOU RATHER

HAVE ALIENS COME TO EARTH
OR
HAVE OUR SPACESHIPS GO TO ALIEN PLANETS?

DISCOVER THAT ALIENS ARE ON EVERY PLANET IN THE UNIVERSE
OR
THAT LIFE ON OTHER PLANETS DOESN'T EXIST?

WOULD YOU RATHER

SPEAK AN ALIEN LANGUAGE
OR
LEARN AN EXISTING LANGUAGE YOU DON'T KNOW?

HAVE ALIENS INVADE EARTH AND RULE US
OR
INVADE AN ALIEN PLANET AND RULE THEM?

WOULD YOU RATHER

MEET AN ALIEN SPECIES THAT LOOKS EXACTLY LIKE HUMANS
OR
ONE THAT LOOKS LIKE A BIG BLOB?

DISCOVER ALIENS IN OUR SOLAR SYSTEM
OR
FIND THEM IN A DISTANT GALAXY?

WOULD YOU RATHER

GET TURNED INTO AN ALIEN
OR
BE BEST FRIENDS WITH ONE?

FIND OUT THAT YOUR PARENTS ARE SECRETLY ALIENS
OR
THAT YOUR FAMILY PET IS A SECRET ALIEN?

WOULD YOU RATHER

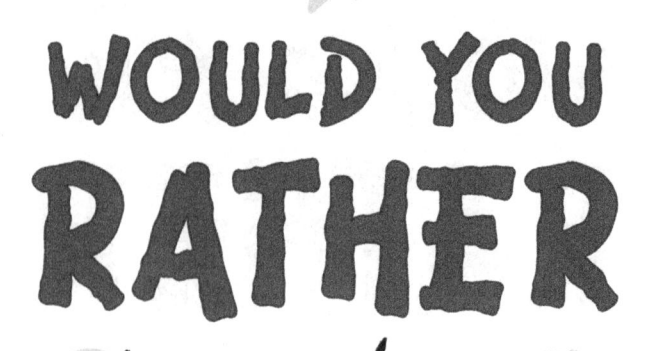

GO TO A SCHOOL WHERE YOU'RE THE ONLY HUMAN STUDENT
OR
TO A SCHOOL WHERE THERE'S ONLY ONE ALIEN STUDENT?

MEET ALIENS WHO ONLY SPEAK IN VOWELS
OR
ALIENS WHO ONLY SPEAK IN CONSONANTS?

WOULD YOU RATHER

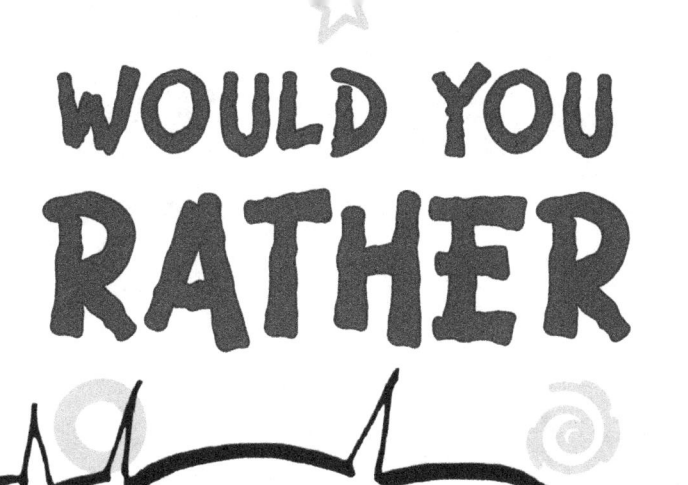

DISCOVER ALIENS LIVING ON MARS
OR
DEEP UNDERGROUND ON EARTH?

MEET A SPECIES OF ALIEN THAT
CAN SHAPESHIFT
OR
ONE THAT CAN FLY?

WOULD YOU RATHER

BECOME AN ALIEN
OR
JUST MEET THEM?

HAVE A UNIVERSAL TRANSLATOR SO YOU CAN SPEAK ALL ALIEN LANGUAGES
OR
A TELEPORTER SO YOU CAN VISIT ALL ALIEN PLANETS?

WOULD YOU RATHER

FIND AN ALIEN CIVILIZATION THAT CAN ONLY BARK LIKE DOGS
OR
ONE THAT CAN ONLY POINT AT PICTURES TO COMMUNICATE?

DISCOVER ALIENS BY THEM COMING TO EARTH
OR
BY US GOING TO THEIR PLANET?

WOULD YOU RATHER

MEET AN ALIEN SPECIES THAT CAN READ EACH OTHER'S MINDS
OR
ONE THAT CAN MOVE OBJECTS WITH THEIR MINDS?

HAVE AN ALIEN BECOME YOUR ADOPTED SIBLING
OR
YOUR STEPPARENT?

WOULD YOU RATHER

DISCOVER ALIENS THAT HAVE FOUR ARMS
OR
ONES THAT HAVE SIX EYES?

MEET AN ALIEN SPECIES THAT ONLY COMMUNICATES WITH MATH
OR
ONE THAT ONLY COMMUNICATES WITH ADJECTIVES?

WOULD YOU RATHER

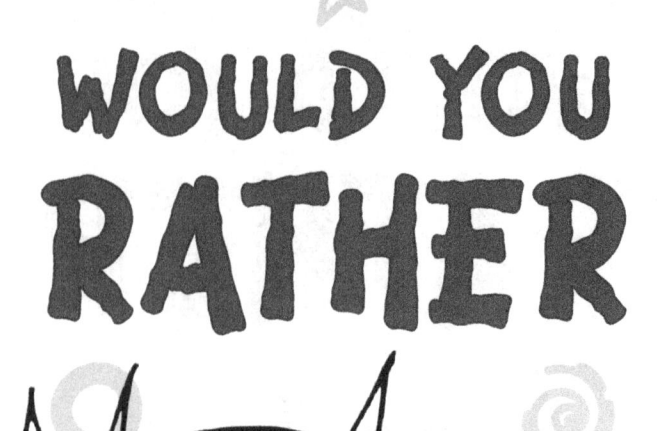

FIND AN ALIEN PLANET FULL OF KIDS
OR
ONE WITH ONLY ADULTS?

INTRODUCE AN ALIEN TO EARTH FOOD
OR
EAT AN ALIEN'S FOOD THAT'S NOTHING LIKE FOOD ON EARTH?

WOULD YOU RATHER

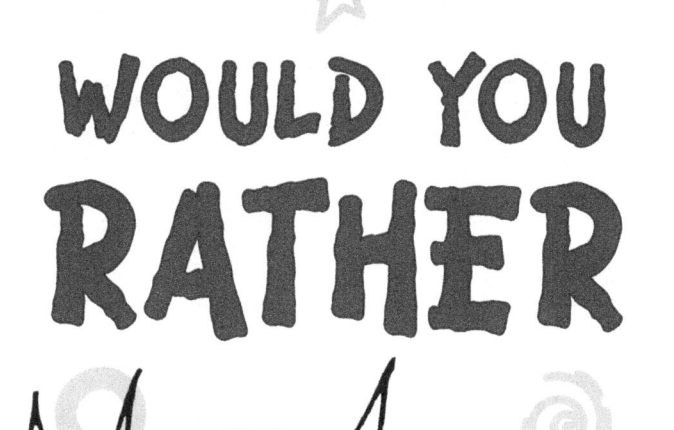

DISCOVER THAT ALIENS BUILT THE PYRAMIDS OF GIZA
OR
THAT ALIENS BUILT THE WHITE HOUSE?

HAVE YOUR BEST FRIEND BE TURNED INTO AN ALIEN
OR
ONE OF YOUR PARENTS TURN INTO ONE?

WOULD YOU RATHER

MEET AN ALIEN WHO THINKS YOU LOOK GROSS
OR
MEET AN ALIEN WHO YOU THINK LOOKS GROSS?

PLAY HIDE-AND-SEEK WITH AN ALIEN THAT CAN TELEPORT
OR
PLAY "THE FLOOR IS LAVA" WITH AN ALIEN THAT CAN FLOAT?

WOULD YOU RATHER

MAKE A SPORTS TEAM MADE ENTIRELY OF SUPER TALL ALIENS PLAY BASKETBALL
OR
FOOTBALL?

DISCOVER AN ALIEN SPECIES THAT HAS NO LAWS
OR
ONE THAT HAS SO MANY LAWS THEY CAN'T REMEMBER THEM ALL?

WOULD YOU RATHER

MEET ALIENS WHO ARE TEN FEET TALL
OR
ONES THAT ARE TEN FEET WIDE?

DISCOVER ALIENS LIVING ON MERCURY
WHO ARE IMMUNE TO HEAT
OR
DISCOVER ALIENS ON PLUTO WHO
ARE IMMUNE TO COLD?

UNIVERSE

WOULD YOU RATHER

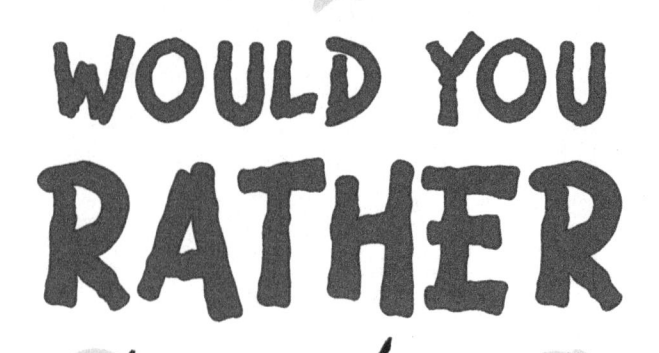

FIND A GALAXY WHERE ALL OF THE PLANETS ARE FORESTED
OR
ONE WHERE ALL OF THE PLANETS ARE OCEANS?

DISCOVER A PLANET WITH ONLY CATS
OR
ONE WITH ONLY DOGS?

WOULD YOU RATHER

FIND THE PLACE IN THE UNIVERSE WHERE GRAVITY IS THE STRONGEST
OR
THE PLACE WHERE IT'S THE WEAKEST?

DISCOVER A GALAXY THAT ONLY HAS ONE PLANET IN IT
OR
A GALAXY THAT HAS SO MANY BLACK HOLES IT'S IMPOSSIBLE TO COUNT?

WOULD YOU RATHER

GO THROUGH A BLACK HOLE
OR
A WORMHOLE?

SEE A STAR FORM
OR
SEE ONE DIE?

WOULD YOU RATHER

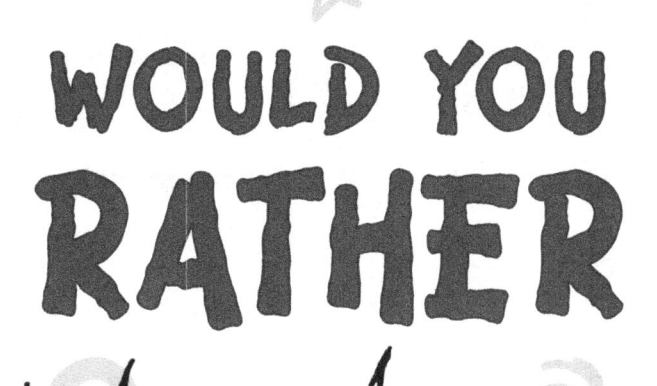

DISCOVER THAT THE UNIVERSE IS INFINITE
OR
THAT IT HAS AN ENDING POINT?

TRAVEL TO THE FARTHEST GALAXY
FROM THE MILKY WAY
OR
TO THE CLOSEST?

WOULD YOU RATHER

GO TO A PLANET WITH TOO MUCH GRAVITY
OR
ONE WITH TOO LITTLE?

HAVE A NEBULA NAMED AFTER YOURSELF
OR
AFTER A GALAXY?

WOULD YOU RATHER

EXPLORE THE EDGE OF THE MILKY WAY
OR
THE CENTER OF IT?

LIVE ON THE HOTTEST PLANET
IN THE GALAXY
OR
THE COLDEST ONE?

WOULD YOU RATHER

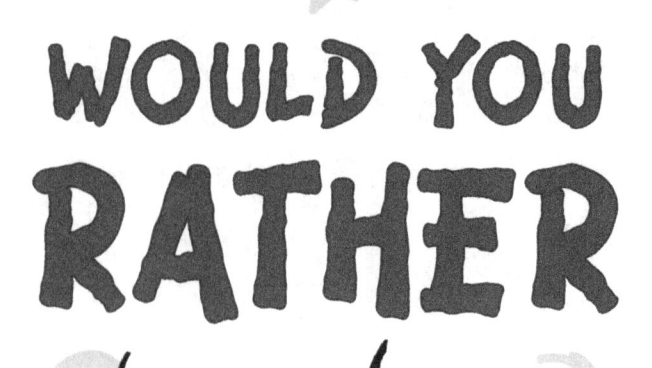

FIND A GALAXY THAT ONLY HAS STARS
OR
ONE THAT ONLY HAS ASTEROIDS?

DISCOVER A STAR SO YOU CAN NAME IT AFTER YOURSELF,
OR
DISCOVER A GALAXY AND NAME IT AFTER YOUR FAVORITE FICTIONAL CHARACTER?

WOULD YOU RATHER

DISCOVER A GALAXY THAT'S SHAPED LIKE A PERFECT CIRCLE
OR
ONE THAT IS SHAPED LIKE A SPAGHETTI NOODLE?

HAVE EARTH BE VERY CLOSE TO ANOTHER GALAXY THAT YOU CAN SEE IT DURING THE DAY,
OR
SO FAR AWAY THAT YOU CAN ONLY SEE THE MILKY WAY?

WOULD YOU RATHER

HAVE THE UNIVERSE EXPAND UNTIL EVERYTHING IS TOO FAR AWAY,
OR
CONTRACT UNTIL ALL OF THE GALAXIES ARE RIGHT ON TOP OF EACH OTHER?

DISCOVER THAT THE WHOLE UNIVERSE CAN FIT INTO THE PALM OF AN ALIEN'S HAND
OR
FIND OUT THAT IT'S ALL A DREAM?

WOULD YOU RATHER

BE IN CHARGE OF THE BEST TELESCOPE IN THE WORLD
OR
BE AN ASTRONAUT ON A ONE-WAY TRIP TO OTHER GALAXIES?

WATCH TWO STARS CRASH INTO EACH OTHER
OR
TWO PLANETS CRASH INTO EACH OTHER?

WOULD YOU RATHER

DISCOVER A VOLCANO THAT TAKES UP AN ENTIRE PLANET
OR
A PLANET WITH ONE GIANT EARTHQUAKE?

LIVE ON A PLANET NEXT TO A BLACK HOLE
OR
ON A PLANET WITH NO WATER?

WOULD YOU RATHER

TRY TO FLY A SPACESHIP THROUGH
A FIELD OF STARS
OR
A FIELD OF BLACK HOLES?

BE THE FIRST PERSON TO DISCOVER
A STAR
OR
THE FIRST PERSON TO DISCOVER
A GALAXY?

WOULD YOU RATHER

VISIT THE SMALLEST STAR IN THE UNIVERSE
OR
THE BIGGEST ONE?

GET TRAPPED IN A NEBULA
OR
IN AN EXPLODING STAR?

WOULD YOU RATHER

FIND THE PERFECT CENTER OF
THE UNIVERSE
OR
THE EDGE OF IT?

TURN A DOZEN STARS INTO ONE
GIGANTIC STAR
OR
A DOZEN PLANETS INTO ONE
GIGANTIC PLANET?

WOULD YOU RATHER

WATCH THE UNIVERSE BE CREATED IN THE BIG BANG
OR
WATCH IT DIE?

INVENT THE BEST TELESCOPE EVER
OR
THE BEST SPACESHIP EVER?

NIGHT SKY

WOULD YOU RATHER

DISCOVER A CONSTELLATION THAT LOOKS LIKE ONE OF YOUR PARENTS
OR
ONE THAT LOOKS LIKE YOUR PET?

ONLY BE ABLE TO FIND YOUR WAY AROUND USING THE STARS
OR
USING A COMPASS?

WOULD YOU RATHER

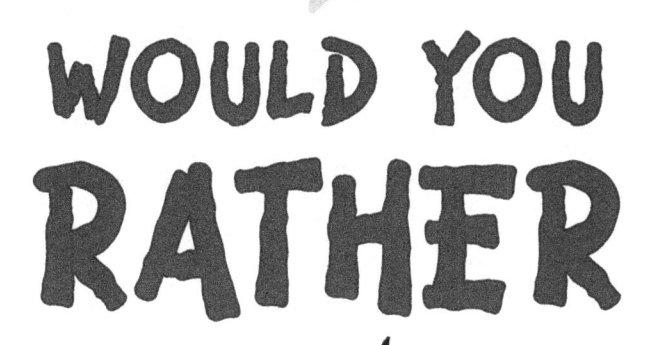

KNOW THE NAMES OF EVERY CONSTELLATION IN THE SKY
OR
KNOW THE NAME OF EVERY STAR IN THE SKY?

MEET THE BEAR FROM THE BIG DIPPER
OR
THE BEAR FROM THE LITTLE DIPPER?

WOULD YOU RATHER

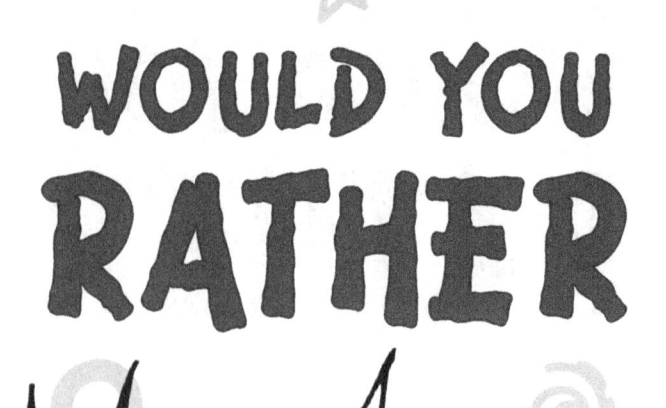

MEMORIZE YOUR STAR SIGN
OR
YOUR BIRTHSTONE?

DISCOVER A CONSTELLATION ALL
ON YOUR OWN
OR
BE ABLE TO POINT OUT EXISTING
ONES IN THE SKY?

WOULD YOU RATHER

BE ABLE TO SEE ALL OF THE STARS WITHOUT A TELESCOPE BUT YOU CAN'T SEE DURING THE DAY,
OR
BE ABLE TO SEE DURING THE DAY BUT UNABLE TO SEE ANY STARS AT NIGHT?

MEET THE BULL FROM TAURUS
OR
THE LION FROM LEO?

WOULD YOU RATHER

HAVE STARS ROTATE AROUND THE EARTH
OR
HAVE THE EARTH ROTATE AROUND ALL OF THE STARS?

FIND A CONSTELLATION THAT LOOKS LIKE YOUR FAVORITE FOOD
OR
ONE THAT LOOKS LIKE YOUR FAVORITE CARTOON CHARACTER?

WOULD YOU RATHER

MEET PERSEUS
OR
HERCULES FROM THEIR CONSTELLATIONS?

SEE THE NORTHERN LIGHTS NO MATTER
WHERE YOU LIVE
OR
BE ABLE TO SEE THE PLANETS OF THE
SOLAR SYSTEM AT ALL TIMES?

WOULD YOU RATHER

BE ABLE TO SEE THE SUN ROTATING
OR
BE ABLE TO SEE EARTH ROTATING?

SWITCH DAY AND NIGHT WHERE YOU LIVE
OR
SWITCH THE NORTHERN AND SOUTHERN HEMISPHERES?

WOULD YOU RATHER

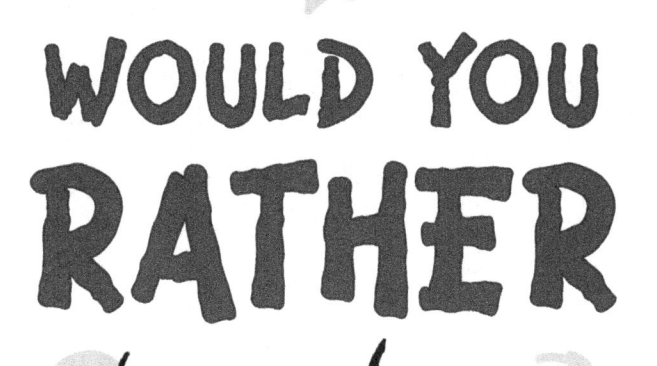

BE ABLE TO TELL WHAT DAY IT IS JUST
BY LOOKING AT THE STARS
OR
BE ABLE TO TELL WHAT TIME IT IS BY
LOOKING AT THE DAYTIME SKY?

MEET THE FLYING HORSE FROM PEGASUS
OR
THE DOLPHIN FROM DELPHINUS?

WOULD YOU RATHER

NAME A CONSTELLATION AFTER YOUR FIRST NAME
OR
AFTER YOUR LAST NAME?

HAVE IT PITCH BLACK OUTSIDE AT NIGHT SO YOU CAN SEE THE MILKY WAY
OR
HAVE LIGHTS ON AT NIGHT BUT YOU CAN ONLY SEE THE BRIGHTEST STARS?

WOULD YOU RATHER

LIVE NEXT TO A POWERFUL TELESCOPE
ON EARTH
OR
LIVE ON A TELESCOPE IN SPACE?

ADOPT THE BIG DOG FROM CANIS MAJOR
OR
THE LITTLE DOG FROM CANIS MINOR?

WOULD YOU RATHER

DISCOVER A CONSTELLATION THAT LOOKS LIKE A CAR
OR
ONE THAT LOOKS LIKE AN AIRPLANE?

HAVE EVERY STAR IN THE UNIVERSE BE A PART OF A CONSTELLATION
OR
HAVE NO CONSTELLATIONS AT ALL?

WOULD YOU RATHER

MEET THE TWINS FROM GEMINI
OR
THE CRAB FROM CANCER?

FIND A CONSTELLATION IN THE SHAPE
OF A SPIDER
OR
IN THE SHAPE OF A GHOST?

WOULD YOU RATHER

WATCH A METEOR SHOWER THROUGH A TELESCOPE
OR
LOOK AT SATURN'S RINGS WITH THAT TELESCOPE?

SEE ALL OF THE CONSTELLATIONS IN THE NORTHERN HEMISPHERE
OR
ALL OF THE ONES IN THE SOUTHERN HEMISPHERE?

WOULD YOU RATHER

LOOK AT STARS IN A TRADITIONAL TELESCOPE
OR
LOOK AT THE SUN THROUGH A SOLAR TELESCOPE?

NAME A METEOR AFTER YOUR FAVORITE SUPERHERO
OR
NAME A CONSTELLATION AFTER YOUR BEST FRIEND?

WOULD YOU RATHER

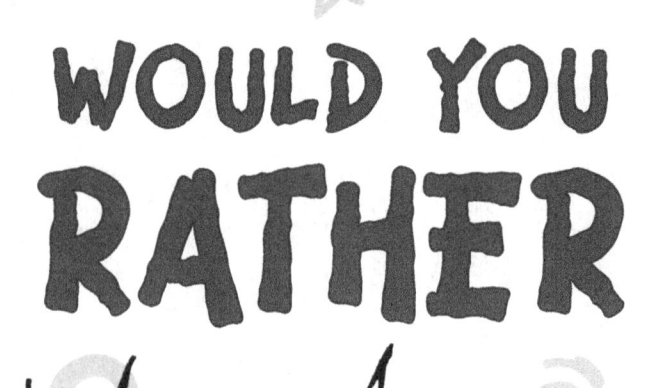

DISCOVER A CONSTELLATION SHAPED LIKE MACARONI
OR
ONE SHAPED LIKE A PIECE OF CHEESE?

MEET THE CENTAUR FROM CENTAURUS
OR
THE UNICORN FROM MONOCEROS?

Made in United States
Orlando, FL
22 July 2024